PROLOGUE

This is a book about alcohol, the good and bad of it and the reality of dependency. This is not a fictional story of how someone was down on their luck and turned to drink, it is about how real life people can slip into drink dependency without ever realising it.

This hopefully, also a book that through sharing my story can help someone step off the merry-go-round of numbness, that we need to cope sometimes and give ourselves some peace.

I cannot promise that this book will cure you of the demons inside your head, nor can I promise peace and tranquillity, but what I can promise you is a true to life, warts and all, brass tacks account of my own personal trip through madness, my focus and clarity today and how I have gotten here.

If this helps just one person, my intention has been successful.

CHAPTER 1

Once Upon a Time

I was 13-14 years old when I first got drunk at my friends house. It was a mixture of homemade damson wine and four cans of Mild, which resulted in my staggering back home, going upstairs to my bedroom and being sick into a carrier bag on and off for an hour and hiding it in my bedside cupboard so Mum and Dad didn't know I had been drinking.

After an hour I had to give up my secret due to the chronic stomach ache I had thanks to an hour of retching. I went downstairs in tears of pan and held my hands up. The reaction I got was not what I was expecting, Mum made me some Indian Brandy with sugar and hot water and rubbed my back, telling me "we've all been there love, I bet you won't do that again, will you?". If only I had listened to those words more carefully, but hindsight is a wonderful thing.

I was around 15 years old when I started going to the pub with the lads as I was already 6"2" and quite stocky as I had discovered weight training at school. I was never into all the football and Rugby lark, it seemed like a lot of effort for no results, plus being tall helped in the 'girl' department. I had a paper round and pocket money which paid for a Friday night on the Town. I did not know how I did it, but I ended up pretty ratted most Friday nights. I think the bottles of 20/20 and White Lightening we drank before going out helped a big with that.

Fast forward to 18-19 years old which consisted of finishing work at 2.00 p.m. on a Friday and the entire factory would descend on the local pub for music, pool, cards, and most importantly beer.

We would go back home and have some tea and get ready for the weekend carnage to begin. From that point it was pretty much a blur until Sunday night. Friday night, Saturday dinner time, Saturday night, Sunday dinner time then the calm down Sunday night. . If anyone missed one or more of these appointments, the ridicule would be almost brutal. Monday morning at work was like a Zombie Apocalypse. Not much got done on a Monday.

By 19 - 20 years old I had found the joys of weed, speed, LSD and Clubbing in the UK and Abroad. I never went overboard with the drugs thing, my poison was alcohol mainly.

At 21 I had met a girl and we were having a baby. The drinking calmed down but never stopped and the occasional joint every now and again. We rented a place and settled into parenthood but alcohol was always there. My routine was already set, but I didn't know it yet, I just thought it was normal to drink every day. The relationship didn't last past 12 months after my son was born as my partner was seeing another man. Neither and both of us were to blame, we parted as friends and still are today. I am very proud of my son and we are now blessed with twin grand-daughters.

After the break-up my drinking in the pubs increased on a social level, to me, it wasn't a problem, more of having friends to talk to.

I spent a few years just being me again, going to concerts, playing in the local pub, Pool and Quiz Leagues and going to Rock Clubs at the local City at a week-end. I used the hair of the dog to get rid of the hangovers, but so was everyone else that I knew and it seemed to work okay. I was finding that when I was drinking , I normally wasn't eating (not a diet I would recommend).

I eventually ended up with a girl who was sort of a friend with benefits, a drunken mutual agreement if you like. We were never actually friends, more the benefit side really. She got pregnant after a while, it was only later that I found out that she had stopped taking her Pill on purpose and not told me. A baby, apparently, can fix a failing relationship, I didn't even know we were in one. Thinking back I should have used protection myself, but we had discussed this, needless to say I stayed around to be a Dad. My second son was born in 1997 and we tried to make it work, but on a holiday to Greece, that her father had paid for, she decided to stay there with a barman she had met. So I lost my son. That is when I think I had my breakdown, I started drinking Vodka to knock myself out. As soon as I woke up I would gulp more down to knock myself out again. I didn't want to wake up. Living in a tent helped, as there was nobody to stop me killing myself, unfortunately my body thought otherwise.

It took me about two and a half years of going through the courts to get any access to my son, but it was worth it. I had since moved on and resumed what I class as a normal life. Social drinking every evening, and I had also met the woman that is now my Wife. We have a beautiful daughter together and after a lot of years of arguments, pain, loss and doubt I believe we are now at a place where we are happy. We still have our problems, but can deal with them together now, which wasn't always the case . Most of the time we were each other's problem.

Over the years I have been hospitalised, glassed, punched, scratched, knocked out, vomited blood, had Vodka tipped in my eyes and so on and so on. Most of it my own fault, but not all of it. I am now sober, bored, but sober and do not intend to die any time soon. I am not a non drinker, I just choose not to drink. I may feel different tomorrow, but it is not tomorrow yet, it is today and I am happy to be sober today.

I am not here to tell anybody that alcohol is bad, quite the opposite, booze can be brilliant. I have had some of the best times of my life while drunk. It is when it changes from fun to drowning your sorrows, to using it as a coping mechanism, to hating it, but being dependent to the extreme.

I was drinking four cans a night after work to start with, more at weekends and was told to stop because it was a waste of money.

I am the sort of person that does not like to be told what to do so I thought that if I want a drink, I will have a drink. I did not want the nagging so would get dropped off at the shops on the way home from work and get a small bottle of Vodka and drink it while walking home, quick to get down you and stronger than beer. That was my way of thinking. Twenty minutes later I was half soaked and no one was any the wiser, I could hide the effects quite well. I would pop back down the shop a bit later to get whatever came to mind and do the same again. This went on for a while and of course the amount I was drinking increased from half a bottle at a time to three quarters of a bottle to a one litre bottle. I started sneaking it in pop bottles at work with a some orange or blackcurrant squash in it and of course packets full of Extra Strong Mints and Chewing Gum.

I eventually got caught and sacked. This obviously had a massive impact on my marriage but I was too far in at this point and used it to dull the pain again. Back to self destruct mode.

Over the years my marriage has been on the edge of the cliff more times that I can remember. I have been kicked out, I have left, I have been removed, I have caused upset, worry and anger to my Wife, my Kids, Parents and Friends over the years which I will never be able to correct. What is done is done but it has not always been helped by the people who think they are helping. I have found that people that are not

Alcohol Dependent feel that the 'tough love' approach is most effective but what it is really doing is making someone who feels that they have no self worth and hates having to rely on this poison just to cope with whatever has driven them to such a low point that they could not see any other way out, is making them feel even lower, which makes us panic. If we feel that we cannot get any lower we have hit rock bottom, be it from removing any access to money (so having to ask for almost pocket money), using violence or aggression to control you. (I have literally got scars to prove it, but some you cannot see, sometimes they hurt a lot more.) Making someone feel worthless because of their addiction and telling them they are useless.

Stopping you leaving the house alone and throwing accusations at you on your return, This will not help. This will isolate you and make you resent the people that think they are helping you. As I have said earlier, don't tell me what to do, I am more likely to do the opposite.

I have had vile things said to me, purely to hurt me because of the hurt my drinking has caused others, things about my Wife, my Children, my Parents and almost everyone I love or have loved and also by these people.

I understand that living with a drunk was probably hell on earth, but nobody wanted to know why I drank, just why I did not stop. There are so many underlying things that make up an unhappy drunk and I hated being tied to it so strongly, but when I drank myself unconscious it was like flicking an off switch in my head. I did not have to think anymore, I could bury my head in the sand because I could not cope with my life, my depression, I just wanted to be switched off.

Taking anti-depressants and drinking was not one of my cleverest ideas. My mood swings seemed to revolve around a six to eight week period. I would have two weeks where I was completely manic and would happily build a house in day, then two weeks of being relatively normal, then two weeks of terrible depression where I struggled to leave the house and would keep the curtains shut and not answer the door. Then back to normal for two weeks before the manic two weeks started again. This went on for years until a Counsellor I was seeing said 'get yourself checked for Bi-Polar disorder'. This I did through the local Mental Health Community team which consisted of walking into a room, explaining my pendulum style mood swinings and history to be told five minutes later "I could tell you were not Bi-Polar from the moment you walked in". So no answers there then, I will never get that time back. so that is skimming over the top of my life so far but there is much more to being sober today than waking up one morning and just deciding not to drink, although people believe it is that easy. Some people will say "STOPPING IS EASY"

CHAPTER 2

Merry-Go-Round

The hardest part of being addicted to alcohol and wanting to be free of it was what I call the Merry-Go-Round, which is drinking to cope and not coping because of the drink. It is very similar to the saying "I eat because I am unhappy, and I am unhappy because I eat" from one of my favourite films. I found myself drinking when life would get so unbearable that I thought that if I did not shut myself off I would end up doing something stupid and ending up six feet underground. So to me it was a quick fix to stopping myself losing control. What I was effectively doing was giving myself a short time to stop everything, unfortunately this involved drinking enough to pass out. Spirits are very good at doing this, but what I was doing was making everything much worse.

I would wake up so hung over that I felt like I was going to die (a litre of spirits at a time will do this to you). I could not eat anything because I felt so sick, I would just bring it back up. I had a choice to make.

1. I could go 'Cold Turkey' and rid my body of all the toxins, which I later found out is highly dangerous as the amount I was consuming could cause me to have fits and in some cases this is fatal
2. Bring myself down slowly which involves reducing your daily intake by 10% every three days, but the first three days are very dangerous and you need to have access to a hospital at short notice just in case things start going pear shaped.

3. Go and get some more alcohol and keep the cycle going.

I often chose the third option until my body couldn't take it anymore. I could almost feel it shutting down and I was forced to stop. My body could not take any more alcohol and would make me vomit. This is where you feel like you are in a living hell. You shake because of the withdrawal with the added bonus of panic attacks and anxiety attacks. You cannot sleep because of body temperature fluctuations, one minute you are freezing cold, then sweating and just as you feel like you are dropping off to sleep due to exhaustion, you feel like you get an electric shock and jump awake thinking you are going to die.

Food is out of the question, as you are in so much pain in your stomach and you are frightened to cough in case you are sick due to burning your insides with neat whisky. This for me used to last around 3-4 days and I could lose half to one stone in weight in this time and look like it was ready to call the undertaker. (Not a good diet). The simplest tasks feel huge because you are extremely ill at this point. Making a sandwich for my daughter would sometimes leave me shaking and sweating like I had just run a marathon, but people around you do not see this or do not want to. All they see is a weak person who is absolutely useless and its all "self induced".

I tried reducing my intake per day once but the amount of degradation it made me feel was almost painful. I felt embarrassed that my Wife had to keep going to buy whisky for me which I would keep in a cupboard in the Kitchen, and every time I started to get bad withdrawal symptoms I would just go and have enough to stop the effects, but that was it . I could not drink in front of my Wife, because I was so embarrassed that I had become this poor excuse of a man.

I would try to eat a few biscuits a day, just to have something in my body, but all I had to do was just cough slightly too hard and there it was again. Missions not accomplished. After about three days I would be able to eat small amounts like a slice of dry bread or a tomato, but anything oily or greasy was definitely off the menu.

After my living hell was over, I would swear never to go there again, but life at home would worsen again. It seems through my eyes that when I was acting up everybody clung together and were united, but as soon as I got back to some sort of normality, they all started acting up and falling apart. I thought for a long time that it was just me seeing what I thought was happening due to my state of mind at the time, but today I see that I was not wrong at all. It is almost like I was a distraction to them. If I was not the big thing for everyone to talk about, some other drama had to take my place.

When I could not hold everyone up on my shoulders anymore, I would go through the same "cowards" way out again, back on the Merry-Go-Round. Almost like running back to Mummy because I thought it would make everything better or maybe feeling nothing was better than feeing I like this. So we would go through it all over again at the expense of my family, work, finances, my own confidence or self worth.

I hated alcohol and felt like it was a disease with no cure, a prison - something - or someone that could give you some peace for a moment but would take part of life as payment.

As selfish as this sounds if you want to get off the Merry-go-round for good you have got to ignore everything in your head that says STOP, for your Wife, Husband, Children, Mum, Dad, Work and Money. You have got to ask yourself am I happy being like this and do I want to be alive in six months time.

Step off the Merry-go-Round in your head, walk around it one last time , just for a look at where you have spent so much of your time. Walk over to the controls and switch off the light, pull the plug, turn off the motor. It is time for everyone to go home, the Fairground is closed and all the noise has stopped. Once you realise it is not there anymore it can become simpler to realise it is a place you used to go. You had some good times there at the start but once it became a hindrance the harder it was to get off. It has stopped being exciting now.

Do not give up drinking out of the guilt you are made to feel, give it up because you want to live and be the potential you know you can be. With a clear head you will be amazed just how much inside of you is just waiting to get out.

CHAPTER THREE

Rock Bottom

We need to approach the subject of depression, where it comes from, what can cause it or make it worse and more importantly how to accept and handle it.

It is so easy to get caught up in the cycle of drink because you are depressed and depressed because you drink. I was on antidepressants for about a decade to be honest they took a lot away from me. They made me live in a very grey world, on the plus side I did not get rock bottom depressed but I also did not get happy or excited about anything. Seeing someone dying on the street, or winning the lottery would not really stimulate any emotion in me. It was all very grey. I would also drink whilst taking my tablets which was not a good idea at all, as it would make all those missed emotions come out, but in a very chaotic way. One minute I would be full of anger or energy and five minutes later I would be crying uncontrollably wishing I was dead . I would become very dangerous when I was in this state as I was very unpredictable. It resulted in my trying to cut my own wrists down the vein. I am not sure if it was me just crying out for help or a cowards attempt at a solution, but it was pretty grim either way.

This is just one example of many where my life could have easily have ended through depression. A lot of people expect you to just pull yourself together or "man up", but it is not as simple as that. Most of the time I did not even know why I was so down because when you are depressed it is mainly due to a chemical imbalance in the brain. You do not need to have a reason It is just there like a cloaked figure that drains you of any joy, happiness and energy.

This was very hard on my Wife, children and family to see me like this, and unable to help me. I would sometimes spend days or weeks not getting out of bed and wishing I just would not wake up. People would get angry with me for not helping myself, but I could not see any way out of this. The only way my brain could see was to die.

Being at rock bottom does not give you very many options, but the old saying that you have to hit rock bottom before you can move upwards was very true for me.

My daughter was taken away from us for a week and taken to a respite centre. This was out of our hands and reduced me to nothing. I was lying on the floor in the foetal position, completely broke. I only had one choice, sort "ME" out once and for all.

The last time I had a drink was 5 November 2018 and it will stay that date, but I have got to keep in my head that I am fully entitled to go and get a drink at any time. This helps me as I am making the decision. It gives me confidence in myself and lifts me up. Most importantly it lets me put that middle finger up to everyone out there that are sat waiting for me to fail again. Mostly people in Authority that have the power to bring us all down if I give them what they are waiting for. All I can say to these people is to keep waiting, watch this space because I am taking control back.

My advice to anyone feeling so low that they are blinded by the darkness is to get a perverse pleasure in proving all the doubters in you out there wrong. Trust me they hate it deep down

One of the things that helped me massively was walking up a mountain with my eldest Son. I simply watched a programme on television one night about one of the three highest peaks in the United Kingdom. Scafell Pike, and thought I can do that, so phoned my Son and asked him "do you fancy climbing 3,800 feet up a mountain on Saturday?" to which he replied "Yeah, why not". So that was it. At 4.30 Saturday morning we went, that simple.

We got there at 9.00 a.m. in the sunshine and headed up towards the snowy top through all the mist (which I thought was clouds), The feeling of being in that sort of isolation was the best feeling in the world . It was just you and the mountain, like being on a different planet. I have never felt so calm in my life. We sat on the top at 12.30 in -10 degrees and hid behind a stone wall out of the wind. Three hours up, one and a half hours back down, and could barely walk for three days afterwards, but I would do it again in a heartbeat. It completely centred me. Not just the sense of achievement, more the peace I felt while I was there. That was my calm place and I will go back , although I want to try Snowdon and Ben Nevis first.

I have found that whilst drunk and going through depression, you can be that full in your head that other things can easily end up taking a back seat. It is hard to fit it all in one head to the point that people around you start to think that you simply do not care. It has affected my personal relationships, my work, being the best Dad and Husband I can be, my sex life, my friendships and causing so much worry to my Mum and Dad.

It is a problem when you cannot dig too deep into your emotions for fear of unearthing something you do not want in your life any more. Be patient, tackle them one by one. I imagine I have a battery on my left hand side(like on a phone display) that tells me how much patience I have. Almost like my armour. On my right hand side I have lots of walls holding back all of the things I need to deal with or put right. If my battery if full, I will take few bricks out of a wall and allow a gentle flow and fix what comes through until my battery gets to about half way. Then I will put a brick back to slow it down then when my battery gets to a third, I put all the bricks back in the wall and seal it with cement. I then put my battery on charge until it is full again and I can fix some more things behind the walls. It is a strange way of dealing with things, but it works for me. Just remember, do not let the battery get below a third as you will need that patience to brick the wall back up, and if you cannot do that, it keeps flowing through until you flood and drown.

CHAPTER FOUR

Withdrawal

This is unfortunately something everyone with alcohol dependency will go through. I will not pretend that it is easy, because for me anyway, it was bloody hard. I have been through it more times than I care to remember, which always resulted in me saying to myself, 'I do not ever want to feel like that again'. Then after a week or two the memory starts to fade and as soon as something else happened to stress me to my limit, I would think 'maybe one would not hurt, just to take the edge off the situation', but it was never just one. For years I would tell myself that I could control this, but the end result was always the same.

From the day that my body would not take any more booze by throwing it back out I had no choice but to go cold turkey. The dreaded detox, back into hell again.

I would be greeted by about three days of feeling so sick, I could not even cough, and the thought of eating anything filled me with dread because how my damaged stomach would react to it. I would seem to have no control over my body, temperature one minute, sweating profusely and then freezing cold. The freezing cold was better than the sweating as when I felt too hot I would start having panic attacked which felt like I was going to die young (and there was good chance that I could). I have sat in the garden in my underwear before now in the middle of winter, in an attempt to cool my core temperature down and have also been in hospital because my attempt did not succeed, which resulted in me almost going into a fit which can be fatal.

I still find it astounding that when I was lying in the hospital A and E bed they would not take me to the main hospital fourteen miles away by ambulance (even though I was drifting in and out of consciousness) because I had not actually had a fit yet and asked if I could make my own way there. I could barely stand up, I was sober, but in massive detox.

The thought of speaking to any one horrified me, as I looked and felt so out of sorts. This is when I would shut the curtains and lock the doors so it looked like nobody was home. I would try and take pills to help but could not keep them down. I could not sleep, even though I was mentally and physically exhausted because of the temperature fluctuations and just as I was dropping off it is almost like you have forgotten to breathe and would jolt awake. I would see things that were not there, shadows coming out of the walls, cockroaches all over the floor, ceiling and walls. People's faces would distort in front of my eyes and all number of horrific things that do not make any sense now. My emotions were at an all time low where sometimes I would sit alone on the settee and sob uncontrollably and think if my body and mind were not strong enough to get through this hell I would welcome death.. I sometimes even wished for it.

It is easy to forget how bad things got but I make a point every day to always give it a quick thought and I am just thankful I am not in hell anymore.

The blame culture is an interesting one to deal with when you are going through all of this. Most people will not really want to know how you feel or care for that matter. You will get a lot of comments like 'it is self-induced', 'it is all your own fault', 'I have got no sympathy for you', 'you deserve all you get' and so on. You will also get ripped apart for everything you have done wrong. Some of it you may remember, some of you will not, but this is because other people are hurting and need to take it out it out on someone, and guess who that someone is. It does not matter that you can barely function, this is where they can be very selfish because they do not understand or simply do not want to understand.

You will become the focus of their anger and upset for a while, but it will pass. As the days go by you will feel stronger and stronger until you feel like yourself again, but this is where I used to slip up a lot, you feel over-confident, and almost indestructible and I used to feel that nothing or nobody ruled me, but how wrong I was. I could go from a superhero to a jibbering wreck in the space of a day. Sometimes getting the bottles of whisky I had hidden outside at 6.00 a.m. before anyone got out of bed. I had been sleeping on the settee for quite a while by now and I would have booze stashed all over the place, under settees, in the garage, on top of cupboards and even out of the house in wheelie bins, down alleys covered in leaves, in the woods and in peoples hedges. The harder ones for people to find were the obvious ones in plain view if you like, in the wash basket, in a coat pocket (someone else's coat) or behind the fridge. Most of the time I would get half way drunk and forget where I had hidden the next bottle and would go into a panic if the shops were not open. I would purposely start an argument so I could walk out to get more, the list is endless. But I always came back to the same place.

Pain, misery and disappointment, back in hell at the start of another three days of agony, wondering if my body would shut down on me this time and above all hurting the people I love the most in my life. To this day I cannot comprehend what they have had to deal with, and how many scars I have cut into them, that they will probably carry for a hell of a long time and I do not know if I would have the stamina they all had not to give up on me when I was at my lowest through being drunk, ill, down or all three of these combined. That is a strength that I envy and always will. In the nicest possible way, all of my close family have helped as well as hindered me through all of this, but one day you have to look at yourself in the mirror and understand that the person looking back at you is the one that is going to help you the most, and your job is to give that person the tools and strength to do it. You can make them better than anyone could believe.

CHAPTER FIVE

<u>Self Hygiene and Esteem</u>

When you are in the deepest, darkest depths of Alcohol and Depression, these two things can be hugely affected or at least they were for me. I have never been one to shower every single day, but this part of my life took me to a whole different realm.

My self-esteem would be so low that I just did not care about myself anymore. I would not bath or shower for months on end. I would not shave or brush my teeth which would result in my gums bleeding every time I ate anything and they would become sore and inflamed. My skin would become dry, itchy and blotchy, but I simply did not care. I would become how I felt 'A Mess'. I would resemble something that had just crawled out of the jungle, raised by wolves or some sort of

Neanderthal, full beard, bags under the eyes, pale, dirty and unable to communicate properly.

I would spend most of my time trying to sleep on the settee, getting into bed with my wife was a distant memory, sometimes I was told I was not wanted in the same bed as her, and other times I was blamed for neglecting by not going to bed. The truth is, I did not feel wanted by anyone, but the strange thing is I did not want to be wanted anymore.

I would feel like the scum of the earth. How could anyone care about me. I was just the dirt to be scraped off their shoes and I truly believed I deserved to feel that way, but let me tell you something that took me a long time to work out. My thinking was so wrong, so distorted and so flawed. Nobody should ever feel that low about themselves. No matter who you are or what you have done, there is always a way to be better than you were. You have to draw a line and say 'beyond that line is the past you cannot change what has already happened.'.

You can however fix things that have got broken in the past, everything can be repaired, it is just having the knowledge to fix it. Just remember the battery life and you walls from Chapter Three. Control the flow of what you can handle and keep an eye on your battery level. Remember, never let it go below a third, all that needs repairing will be fixed but do not try to rush it or you will make mistakes. Put those bricks back in the wall when you need to, you are the one in control, you choose how fast the flow is and you can stop it all when 'You' want. You are the boss.

Do not fall into the same trap that I did, thinking that you are a disgrace because things are slipping away from you. You are not going to die if you do not have a wash, brush your teeth, answer the door or open the curtains. It will come in its own time. Do it at your pace and not anybody else's. When you start to see that glimmer of light, do not take your eyes off it, and it will grow bigger. Once you get that, the rest will follow. Backwards will not become an option to you anymore, you will start to see where you want to be and will start planning how you are going to get there. From time to time you might go back to your Merry-Go-Round just for a look (when you feel strong enough). I have been to mine in my head a few times, the first time it was just derelict, covered in leaves, broken lights and flaking paint. It looked like it had not worked since I last switched it off and it was decayed. There was no fairground anymore. The Merry-Go-Round just stood alone an empty field, it was raining and windy and I was glad I did not have to stay there anymore.

The last time I went it was even standing anymore, it was just a pile of wood and metal that did not have a use anymore.

Some people might think I am mad to imagine all of this in my head, but it helped me and I am here today and I am sober and I am writing a book to give you something I would have given my right arm for when I needed help. The honest truth, and if you can take anything from this book and use it to help you that makes me extremely happy.

I promised myself and my loved ones so many times that I had stopped for good or I would die and I did believe myself at the time. (I was going to pick my life up because it was the only that thing would save me.) I am often asked why, the last time I said this was actually the last time and why was it different to all the other times and I honestly do not know. Something clicked inside of me, my whole way of thinking just changed in a matter of seconds. When the Authorities took my daughter away from us for her own good, my life imploded in on me, but

I went out and got drunk to cope with it. After a week we got our daughter back, but my wife and I separated for a short while so my drinking was not a threat to my daughter. I stayed in a friends caravan for a week, no electric, no gas, no heating, just me. November 5th was the last time I drank alcohol in that caravan. Whatever it was that clicked in me happened that night, listening to the torrential rain on the roof, pitch black darkness and freezing cold. I walked up and down the canal side just down the road and thought very deeply about what would be best for everyone. My wife phoned me just before the battery ran out on my phone and I told her I thought it would be best if I was not around anymore for my daughters sake. Everybody that was supposedly there to help us had already put the idea there in my head, social workers, school workers and many other people with the power to insist that my daughter needed better care.

So I had a choice, how do I leave the people I love with everything in my body and soul. Do I jump in the canal, move away, get myself put in prison, drink myself to death. How could I live without these people in my life based on the opinions of other people who were just doing their jobs to please the boss, to get promoted, but mainly to tick a box.

That was my true crossroads in life, that point in time. in that moment, that second. For some reason nothing that anybody thought mattered to me anymore. I threw the empty bottle in the canal and just watched it bob up and down. That was it. I did not need that stuff anymore. I wanted to live, and be a Dad and Husband and be successful. I was going to treat my family to holidays and make real memories and most of all I was going to prove everyone wrong about me. I am a good bloke underneath all the silt. It was time to do some dredging and let the real me come back up to the surface.

I have also found that a lot of people like to doubt your sobriety. The same people that liked to put you down when you were already at the bottom, almost seem to get upset when you start to rise higher and higher. It is almost like they boosted themselves up by putting you down, somehow making their lives better by feeling that they were above you and always saying 'I wonder how long until the next time'. I get so much pleasure out of watching them squirm as I rise higher and higher and higher. I surpassed many of them a long time ago and see how many insecurities they have in their own lives. I could point all their flaws out but would that not make me exactly what I hated about them. I am far better than that. I will just keep going upwards and getting better and better. When I was at my crossroads I felt like I had just two roads in front of me, one had death at the end of it, and if I chose that one I was going to run as fast as I could to get to the end of it and nothing would stop me. Get to the end point as quickly as possible. The other had no end so anything could be over the horizon. It could be good or bad, it could be sunny or raining. It was simply unknown but I am very artistic and inventive. I could make it what I want and so far I am making more improvements day by day, and I am happy to live where I am today and I am going to make the future even better.

CHAPTER SIX

Urges

One of the hardest things to deal with in my own opinion is the split second decision when deciding to remain sober. It is not always a planned out thing, when you get your next bottle, can, pint or short. Most of my failings have happened from out of nowhere. I have been going to the local shop to get bread, milk, chocolate or cigarettes and when paying for them I have just glanced at the shelf behind the cashier and heard myself saying "oh and a small bottle of whisky as well please". These are the ones to be careful of, as they creep up on you, almost like instinct and before you know it you are glugging back a half litre bottle on the way back home. With me, one is never enough has you have probably guessed by now.

I was known at my local shop as Mr Whisky to all the staff and to a lot of the customers, never to my face obviously, because they would lose my custom but people talk and everything gets back in the end. So I would alternate between different shops to try and avoid the shame I felt.

Sundays were always a problem to me as the shops would not sell booze before 10.00 a.m. and if had not got a bottle stashed somewhere I would start to panic and the withdrawal would start.

When you hit your own crossroads you need to rethink everything that you used to think controlled you. Alcohol is everywhere and it is not going away. Just remember that it is only your problem and not everyone's. There are thousands of other things on the shelves and that bottle or can staring back at you is no more of a threat than anything else in the shop. Do not give it taboo status, it works, teach yourself to deglamorise it, I still think to this day that if I want a drink I will have a drink. I am old enough, I am not breaking any laws, I am fully entitled to. I choose not to. I do not want to be back where I was for so long, I have wasted enough of my life being sad, unhappy and controlled. Not anymore.

Keep in your head that you are stopping for you, not for anyone else. Let everyone stand by and watch how high you can fly. The feel of proving everyone wrong is a very good feeling and I use that a lot to drive me because , let's face it, everybody likes to be right. It is most likely I feed off watching people get annoyed that I have still not slipped backwards. Yes it is an odd way to think about things, but I am a better person because of my stubbornness and my refusal to conform to everybody's expectations.

When people told me to stop, I would do it even more, but now I do not do it because I have chosen not to. These people are still getting what they wanted, but I always make sure they know this is all my doing, not theirs. If anything they drove me deeper into the silt that covered my life. Remember, this is all you and you do not need to thank anyone for their help, their patience, maybe, but you are the one responsible for you still being alive today.

My new addiction is chocolate, not a healthy option I know, but no where nearly as destructive as booze. I am also trying to qualify as ice cream eater of the year and it's safe to say I am putting in plenty of training. I have quite a physical job so can manage to work off the pounds quite easily. It is all about balance.

I still go to counselling sessions for numerous things, a Drinks Counsellor, General Counsellor and I am still seeing my Probation Officer. All of which I now consider friends. I am seeing my Probation Officer because I decided to sleep off a binge session in my friend's car, and I had the keys on me, so was arrested for drunk in charge of a vehicle. (I still not cannot figure out how you can be in charge if you are unconscious).

Emma, Tina and Jess have been wonderful and have listened to me rather than try and direct me. Tina was just a Counsellor, I tried, working for the same Company as my Drinks Counsellor, and she has helped me so much I can never repay her. She likes and understands my visualisations and she sees how I am improving every week. The meetings that we have are directed by me and there are no forms to fill out. It is just a great place to talk about anything without judgement. I wish I had met ~Tina years ago. My life may have been different.

I

CHAPTER SEVEN

Family and Friends

The hard truth is that the people that love you the most are the ones that can cause the most pain. They can run you down without realising how much it can be hurting you but they feel a lot of resentment because when you have been vacant for whatever amount of time, they are the ones trying to hold everything together and they have to come to terms with the fact your death is lurking just around the corner. That amount of frustration can and will erupt and manifest itself in some of the most horrible way.. I have taken physical , emotional and verbal abuse for quite a time from people close to me because they cannot understand that it is an illness but you cannot just take a pill and feel better. This illness causes as much pain for them as it does for you and in their eyes, you are the cause.

I have been told so many times how much of a failure I am by so many people and they will use anyone or anything to cause you as much pain as possible. Kids are a good weapon to use for some people they cause you the most hurt. When these things are said to you and you are a very low point in life, they can hurt tenfold and can drive you to the point where you consider if taking your own life would save everyone from anymore pain or suffering. Whenever I have been at this point in my life I have always had this voice in my head that says 'you cannot do this to your kids, they love you no matter what'. I do not know where this voice of reason comes from in a head full of chaos, but it is right, your kids deserve only the best of you and I want my Kids to be better and happier than me in every way. Ending your life will ruin them, not help them and to this day I have tried to support and love my kids as much as is humanly possible and I now get it back as well.

You will go through a patch when you believe that everybody hates you but they believe that the things they are doing are because they love you and do not want you to die. This is an awkward stalemate because what they are doing is taking everything away from you and it feels like you are being kept in a cage like some sort of prisoner with no rights whatsoever.

This made me want to escape the cage even more and when I did escape I made of the most of it before I got caught again. The interesting thing is nobody ever asked me how they could help. To me they all had their own theory on how they could stop me but when their little experiments failed they would just cast me out into the gutter and carry on with their merry little lives. I was the failed experiment lying in the gutter in pieces and I had to put myself back together yet again. All I wanted was for somebody to ask me "how do you want to do this?" and I knew the answer all along but did not realise it. Stop trying to cage me and I will stop trying to escape;

I have lost some very close friends through drink, from car accidents and to liver failure. My first loss was my best friend as a child, We were like brothers growing up and when we got older we split off into our respective groups. I always said 'hi' and had a chat when I saw him. We were still good mates, he was always polite to everyone. One day I found out that he had been offered a liver transplant, but I never knew his drinking was that bad. It turns out he refused the transplant because he knew he would wreck that one too and said it should go to someone who really needed it.

He died at 28 years old, leaving a son and girlfriend. I helped to bury him on that day it still breaks my heart now. I will always miss him dearly. Others I have known have died in car accidents on their way home and I had to help drag my friends body out of the car and someone else who died as a result of trying to stop drinking, to fast which turned out to be fatal.

Because of my driving conviction I had to attend a Drink Impaired Drivers Programme once a week for fourteen weeks and hated the thought of it. But I made a lot of good friends on that course and got such a lot out of it which I was not expecting. All of the people running the course were fantastic to work with and were not anti-drink at all. At the end of the course I was glad to get my Saturdays back, but was also sorry for it to end as we had some great laughs and learnt a lot.

All of the people that ran me down when I was at my lowest, for some reason almost do not like the fact that I am not drinking now. It is like they boosted themselves up by putting me down and they often say "It is only a matter of time" or "he's sober now, until the next time" and the more I do not do it the more they seem to squirm which I use as a driving force, I think you to have that side to you.

When I say that I am the one who stopped me drinking, I really mean it. When everyone had had their go at stopping me and failed I had to think to myself I cannot keep getting used and cast aside like this anymore. You can only repair yourself so many times before you are unfixable, so I thought I will show them the right way to fix me for good and I do not want anyone interrupting me whilst I am doing it. So that is what I did and the freedom I feel today is something I forgot over all the years, I must have felt like this before at sometime I cannot remember when, it must have got buried with the silt.

CHAPTER EIGHT

Other Addictions

This is where I want to question the addition vs. the substance. In my own personal experience the substance could have been anything, the addiction on the hand was a mindset where your addictive personality tells you that you cannot live without it or control it for that matter. Do people who have an addiction to food, drugs, phones, violence, etc have the same type of chains tied to them and is it as hard to break free of those chains.

In my opinion, the addictive mind is harder to break free of, than the substance, you almost have to relearn yourself how to think about things, to deglamorise the substance, that is so powerful to you. I do not fear being left alone around alcohol anymore because I do not want to drink it for me. I do not want the chaos it can cause anymore and yes, it would lead to more than one with me. My life today far outweighs the buzz I would get from that feeling of being drunk, but I am the one that has made my life this way, and I want more of it.

I know people who are addicted to food that seem to blame it on everything or anyone for that substance but by far the worst addiction I see at the moment is mobile phones. Yes they are part of our lives but they are taken to a whole new level with people these days, when you see people go into a panic if their battery dies, or heaven forbid, they lose their phone. I recognise this panic and it is just the same as what I had when I could not see the next bottle. I have even had to spend £50 on a second hand phone to tide someone over until a replacement phone gets to them. It is the excuse for needing the phone that I can see through more than anything, as I have done this myself with alcohol. The addiction is the same, the focus of that addiction is the only thing that is different.

I have often wondered what would happen if the internet failed and there was no given time of repair, would the streets be filled with anarchy because at the moment it seems to be filled with zombies, slaves to that thing in your hand. I see Mums and Dads walking the kids to school, pushing prams across the road and hardly ever looking up from their phone to see if the little ones are still in sight or judging whether that car has stopped to let them cross the road. This, to me is allowing the people you love to get in harm's way or get hurt because of your addiction, exactly what I was doing, my substance was just different. Addiction first, loved ones second.

Anything that can make you change your priorities to such a degree can and will cause your life to be turned inside out in the blink of an eye. Adults are telling kids that they need to go out and play with friends instead of being on their phones all the time. Kids learn by example and I do not see many adults practising what they are preaching. When we go out for meals, we watch the people sat around us locked to their phones and not even looking at the person next to them or opposite them, unless they have just shared a post with them of a picture of them all sat round their table, not talking to each other, with the caption 'out with my bffs, having such a great time. Are you really or are just showing people what you want them to see. It is almost like an opium den, everyone is having a great time and everybody is together, but nobody is talking to each other. It is all happening in a fake reality. We are the real people watching what a great time you are really having.

Are all of us addicts, just addicted to this rush of adrenalin or the endorphins released in our brains that we get from whatever the focus of that addiction. I believe we are, the substance is great for a short time and then, when the rush is gone, it is all a big downer which is where the guilt, shame and depressions comes in, so you do it again to try and achieve the same rush. That is when it becomes a dangerous habit.

CHAPTER NINE

Relapse Dream

A few nights ago I had something I call a relapse dream, which can be terrifying as well as extremely upsetting. It had been a normal night at work and home. I had been lying on the settee, watching television when everyone had gone to bed, having 'me' time and nodded off to sleep halfway through whatever I was watching. This is where the nightmare began.

All of a sudden I was in a meeting at my daughters school, but completely drunk. My brain was sober, but I was trapped inside my drunken body. I was slurring my speech, could not walk straight and was so frustrated that I couldn't communicate with the people properly. All of the people there were looking down at me, and telling me what a waste of time I was. People of Authority all telling me I had lost my wife, daughter, sons grandchildren and job. I was trying to tell them this was not the real me but they were telling me they had just been waiting for this to happen.

Then I was out of the meeting with nowhere to go. Nobody wanted me and then the feeling came back, the worst part of this dream, was the uncontrollable urge to get spirits and get as drunk as possible. That familiar fear of not being able to get any, the total need to get back on the Merry-go-Round. I somehow managed to get to a shop where I could get alcohol and when I asked for some, the cashier was looking at me in disgust and shaking their head as they handed me the bottle. Then everybody I love was telling me they wishes I would just hurry up and drink myself to death. All the time I felt like I was stuck in a cage in my head. I did not want any of this, but I was stuck again, underneath all the silt and nobody could see me. All they could see was this horrible mess I was driving around in. Nobody knew I was of sober mind underneath it all. It was a choice of giving into it and being what everyone thought they were looking at or try and fight through all of this fake portrait of me and make the real me surface but that was much harder and would take longer than giving in.

All of a sudden I was woken up by the sound of my alarm going off. At that point I did not know if I had slipped again or if it was a dream. I was in a complete state of panic. I was devastated. What if the dragon had woken up again. Then I realised my head did not feel like it was splitting in half and I did not want to vomit. Thank God, it was a dream, a nightmare, but it unearthed those vile feelings of need, of total dependency again. It made me realise how far I had come and how much I never wanted to go back.

It knocked me about for a few days, revisiting those feelings was a horrible experience, It made me relook at the feeling of worthlessness. I have never been so happy to hear my alarm clock go off in my life, realising that it was my brain playing a cruel prank on me, but it also made me understand that I was there all along and you must never stop swimming towards the surface, because if people cannot see you, they can forget the real you still exists. Be proud of who you can be and let everyone see it. Get from under the silt and show them are still here, then you can start to put right everything that has been left unattended while you have been gone, one brick at a time.

I only write about this because even when you feel confident that you have left your old life behind and everything is on the up, you can still get thrown a curved ball when you do not expect it. So be strong enough to take it on the chin and realise that these things will happen from time to time but you are stronger than a feeling. You are you, and it takes more than that to knock you off the rails. Be proud of that.

For a few days after I was very quiet and when I did join in conversation, I found I was being a bit snappy at home. It was obviously still on my mind so I did what I do not normally do, I spoke to my wife about it and told her I was sorry that I had been grumpy lately but I was not sure why. I explained about the dream and that I had to cope with feelings I did not want anymore. This gave my wife some peace of mind as she knew it was not her I was upset with, it was something invisible and it helped me to talk about how it made me feel. The point I am trying to make is that relapse does not always mean you have returned to taking whatever substance you were chained to, it can also be your mind set, that dependency that took over a your life but you cannot always have control over that, you dream what you subconscious decides, it is fixable.

CHAPTER TEN

Boring Things I know

During my Drink Impaired Drivers' Programme course, apart from meeting a lot of likeminded friends, I actually learnt quite a lot , which I did not expect to do as I was told by a Court of Law to attend for 14 weeks on a Saturday morning. I became friends with the people who ran the course too. They taught me things that I had not really thought about before, as much as I now like having my Saturdays back, I do miss the comradely we had there.

I found out that your body can absorb one unit of alcohol every hour, which means half a pint or one pub shot of whisky per hour. Sounded like a pretty boring night out to me, as my steady average was around two to three pints an hour. One of the questions I asked about this was does the absorption rate reduce as you asleep, because I could sleep for ten hours after a night out still feel the effect the next morning. It turns out that the answer is yes, the body can slow down the absorption rate by about 20% when asleep, which is worth bearing in mind for morning after drives.

We also dealt with the myths around drink driving, such as sucking a copper coin, eating a meal before drinking, drinking black coffee to sober up etc. The copper coin trick I actually used many years ago and it actually worked for me back then, but breathalysers are far more sophisticated now and it does not work anymore. The eating before drinking is a good one, but all does is delay the effects of the alcohol for a short time as your stomach deals with things on a first come first service basis. Almost like a shelf stacking system. Whatever you have consumed before drinking will be dealt with first before it gets to the drink you have put on top of it. I thought it all just went into the same bowl and all got mixed up together, but believe it or not, sometimes even I am wrong. The other one was drinking black coffee which I am sure we have all seen on the television but as we all know coffee can dehydrate you when you are already dehydrated from the alcohol. Your best bet is simply water although in my personal experience, when I have been drinking spirits it has made me feel quite drunk again.

A lot of what we did was talking about how drink can influence your emotions, I am guilty of this in a big way and it is one of the only two comments made on my end of course report and I agree with totally. Managing my emotions is very important and finding alternatives to combat situations has helped me massively. For instance when everything at home turns into World War Three, for whatever reason, I will now take a step back, think and remove myself from the situation, whereas before I would have been in no man's land in the middle of that war trying to fight to win. If you come back after everyone has run out of bullets there is less chance of fatalities.

I cannot thank Helen, Susie, Janet and Les enough for being such great fun as well as informative in something that I thought would be boring and I really did not want to do. I learnt so much and you all helped me to look at a way I could stop and think, make a plan before hand and even during a difficult situation, alter the outcome of that situation. To the rest of the 'offenders' on the course I wish you all the best on your journey. I enjoyed having a laugh with you all and I could not have wished for a better group of people to spend fourteen weeks with (every Saturday). I still think that driving after 5 units or 5 single whiskies is not safe limit to abide by.

I also found out that even though everyone will tell you that the liver is the only organ in the body that can repair itself, what they do not tell say is that it repairs itself with scar tissue or effectively dead tissue, so you will never achieve a perfect liver again, but I am okay with that, the best I can get it, is good enough for me. I also know that when the pull for alcohol can get quite bad, a chocolate bar can ward the edge off for a short period as it releases the same endorphins in the brain as alcohol, mad but true. I have used this method a few times myself and it really works for a quick fix.

The reaction time to stopping in a car going 30 mph from the moment you see the incident to the moment you stop is 15 metres, which we measured out in the corridor and it astounded me how big a distance that was. Just imagine 15 long paces and under the influence your reaction times are slower. This is one of the things that really took me by surprise.

CHAPTER ELEVEN

<u>Final Advice</u>

I wanted to write this book to help anyone who was in the situation I was once in. I do not feel bound by words per page or pages per chapter, as I wanted to get straight to the point and fast. This is not a novel. This is more of a self help novelette if you like and I believe if you need to read this book you want help now, not in three weeks of reading Today.

To be strong enough to be the Commander and Chief over this addiction you have to be selfish for a short while. Imagine you are stood in front of an audience of people made up of everyone you love and hate. You are now going to part these people like Moses, parting the Red Sea, and create a single pathway straight through the middle of them. Now tilt that entire audience upright so you are at the bottom of them and run like you have never run before, straight up that pathway and do not stop until you get to the other end. Those waves of people will close behind you soon and you want to make sure that when this happens you are at the other end, at the top. Do not let anything distract you, no matter who or what it is. Just keep running, everyone's job is to stop you getting to the top so do not give them anything until you are there.

Once you have reached that goal you can let the pathway close up behind you. You are now on top, looking down, you do not have anyone keeping you down there anymore. You are now your own Commander and Chief and you make the rules. If everyone wants to be higher they have got to come through you first because you are now the boss of you.

Make going back down to the bottom an impossibility. You cannot now anyway because the pathway does not exist anymore.

Just remember the bricks in the wall and your battery life and anything is possible to you, you control the flow, one brick at a time. Feel free to go back and have a look at the old broken Merry-Go-Round when you feel comfortable enough. Nobody is telling you to because you are the boss now.

Always remember that you can dazzle people with who you are now. You were always there, but people could not see you before. Just imagine what they have been missing. You were just buried treasure. Show them all what you are really capable of, you never know. Some of them might become quite envious of you, but when I see those people, I remember

'GIVING UP IS EASY THEY SAID'

Thanks to:

Cheryl
Charlotte
Connor
Sam
Mum and Dad
Alex
Tina
Emma
Jess
Helen
Susie
Janet

Les
Gill

You have all helped me in your unique ways.

Thank you

Dan

Printed in Great Britain
by Amazon